MEMORIES OF COVENTRY

ALTON DOUGLAS

DENNIS MOORE

ADDITIONAL RESEARCH BY

JO DOUGLAS

ISBN 0 902464 26 4

Published by Coventry Newspapers Ltd, Corporation Street, Coventry CV1 1FP.

Printed by Tomes of Leamington, 46 Bedford Street, Leamington Spa.

CONTENTS

c/o Circulation Promotions Dept.,
Coventry Evening Telegraph,
Corporation Street,
Coventry CV1 1FP.

Dear Nostalgic,

In the four years since "Coventry at War" was published so much seems to have happened in the world of Alton Douglas Books. The total sales of our local books have moved on towards the 100,000 mark and at this moment you are looking at number eleven in the chain!

Our early researches into Coventry's past unearthed a great many treasures that would not fit into the Second World War concept that we were engaged upon and so, I suppose, "Memories of Coventry" was inevitable.

We have had help from many people and listed on the last page you'll find a "thank you" to all our helpers, but we would like, in particular, to mention the Library Staffs at the Coventry Evening Telegraph and the Local Studies Dept.

I would remind you that we are not historians in the accepted sense of the word but, rather, a trio with an unquenchable enthusiasm for images of the past; an enthusiasm we would like to convey to you through this collection of photographs and advertisements. We have no message to propound, only a desire to entertain.

So — let the entertainment begin!

Yours in friendship,

Alton

ALTON DOUGLAS is probably best known as the quizmaster (and co-writer), for three years, of the top-rated BBC Midlands TV series "Know Your Place," but he is also an after-dinner speaker, author, TV and radio character actor, ex-professional comedian, showbiz/jazz book and record reviewer, TV and radio commercial voice-over artist, one-time 5th Royal Inniskilling Dragoon Guards trombonist, the voice behind several cartoons and children's toys, etc.

He has appeared in virtually every major theatre in the UK (including the London Palladium) and is the veteran of hundreds of television studio warm-ups, but these days specialises in good class hotel, restaurant and conference work, as a sophisticated and highly original humorous after-dinner speaker.

He has been featured as an actor in the TV programmes "Angels," "Seconds Out," "Crossroads," "A Soft Touch" and "Muck and Brass." His other television appearances include "The Golden Shot" (which he hosted on one memorable occasion), "The Knockers," "The Original Alton Douglas," "Nights at the Swan" and "Watch This Space." In 1985 he was featured on television in "The Barmaid's Arms," "Open University," "Property Rites," "Newshound" and "Murder of a Moderate Man." In 1986 he was seen in "Boon" and "Big Deal," recorded his first Radio 4 play "Mr Peabody and the Beast" and commenced his third series of Wednesday big band programmes for Beacon Radio.

Since 1981 Alton has had the following books published:

"Alton Douglas's Know Your Place"
"Birmingham at War Vol. 1"
"Birmingham at War Vol. 2"
"Memories of Birmingham"
"Alton Douglas's Celebrity Recipes"
"Coventry at War"
"The Black Country at War"
"Memories of the Black Country"
"Joe Russell's Smethwick"
"Memories of Shrewsbury"

He also has three books of nonsense verses and a collection of short stories lined up for publication.

INTRODUCTION

BY 1950 (in no small measure due to the effects of the recently ended war) Coventry had changed and grown so swiftly that the modern city was in danger of forgetting the glories and beauty of the old city. As time has moved to the present, it has become even more apparent that memories of the old Coventry are more precious than ever and need to be preserved. This book aims to do just that.

Towards the end of the 1st century AD, there was no settlement of tribes or families in Coventry. The land, being clay, was difficult to work and much of the ancient forest had to be cleared first. In contrast, the sandy soil and tree-free areas of Baginton and Corley were much more hospitable, and it was these that were eventually to grow into the habitation we now know as Coventry.

There are numerous spellings of early and late Coventry including: Cofentreium, Coventreo, Coventria, Coventre, Cofantreo, Coventrev, Couentre, Coventrey, Covingtre and Covintry. The last part of the word certainly suggests a tree and the first part seems to refer to a person named Cofa. Who he or she was and why they planted a tree or inspired the planting of a tree within the ancient settlement remains a mystery. In 1043 Leofric, Earl of Mercia, with his wife, Godiva, founded a monastery in Coventry for an abbot and 24 monks. The king, Edward the Confessor, was greatly in favour and rewarded them both by granting a charter confirming the gift. The real beginnings of Coventry stem from the foundation of this monastery for, as it grew in influence, greater resources were required, so attracting pilgrims, craftsmen and merchants into the community.

No mention of Godiva could fail to include the legend of her famous ride, undertaken to free the local inhabitants from certain taxes levied by her husband Leofric. There is no "Peeping Tom" in the original legend but present-day citizens perpetuate his existence.

Its central situation favoured the growth of Coventry, and the River Sherbourne (at one time much bigger than it is now) provided water supplies and a source of power for the mills. Local stone from Whitley and Cheylesmore assisted building and good, arable land was close at hand for farming and stock-rearing. At the time of the Domesday Book (1086 AD) Coventry was still a very small village containing a mere handful of people but by 1500 AD prosperity was at its height. Cloth, wool, leather and metal goods, soap and needles were the early trades.

When Henry VI visited the town in 1451 he complimented the mayor and burgesses on the excellence of their local governing, urging them to continue this good work and to maintain the peace. The king's parting gift was to confer on Coventry the singular honour of being a county.

By the early 18th century the town was large and well populated, doing great trade in cloth, ribbons, clocks and watches and silk-weaving, the latter remaining a major industry until the invention and manufacturer of bicycles, motor-cycles, motor-cars and areoplanes.

Population growth is significant: under 13,000 in 1749, just over 16,000 in 1801, near 37,000 in 1851 and in 1901 almost 70,000. By 1932, 167,046 inhabited the city, 258,211 by 1951, whilst present numbers exceed 316,000. Boundaries became contentious issues in 1838, resulting in an Act of Parliament (1842) which took away Coventry's status as a county and re-defined the boundaries as a city enclosing 1,486 acres.

On the night of November 14, 1940, a clear, cold, beautiful night, came the greatest air-raid so far directed by the Germans against an English provincial city in the war which had begun in 1939 and was to last until 1945. St Michael's Church, the old Cathedral, was destroyed with only its great tower and spire remaining intact, but by 1962 a new Cathedral, built right against the old, was consecrated. In 1987, for the first time in 100 years, the bells of the old Cathedral rang out officially to mark the 25th anniversary of the event.

Reconstruction of the bomb-scarred city gave opportunities for planners to open up the city to traffic (by use of an inner ring-road) yet at the same time reducing cross-city motor traffic. Further steps were taken to provide pedestrian-only precincts where shoppers were free from motor traffic.

With this post-war planning and the eventual realities came hope for the citizens and workers of Coventry — a hope born out of new industries where the old had become outmoded and a belief that the city would once again hold its head high with pride in the achievements of its craftsmen, its managers and its professions.

BEGINNINGS

UNTIL the early part of the 18th century, education was neither universal nor compulsory and what educational facilities existed were not funded by or controlled by the State. Only the wealthy could afford to pay fees. However, the monks at Leofric's priory, as part of their alms-giving, started a school for poor children. After 1303 the priory also maintained a public grammar school. A typical school day in the summer ran from 6 am to 11 am followed by an afternoon session from 1 pm to 5 pm — quite a rigorous routine. Holidays were brief and occasional half-days were granted for special reasons only. There were no organised games and the main subjects were music and the classics. Charity schools came into prominence between the end of the 17th century and the middle of the 19th century. Among these were three for girls — The Blue Coat School, Southern and Craner's and the Freemen's Orphan School. Foundations for boys were Baker, Billing and Crow's, Katherine Bayley's in Little Park Street and Fairfax's in Spon Street. A School of Design was opened in 1843 with particular reference to the ribbon industry. Twenty years later a School of Art was built in Ford Street.

Fairfax's (Green Gift) School, c. 1887

School band of Katherine Bayley's School (Blue Gift), Little Park Street, c. 1887

Bablake School, c. 1887

Blue Coat School, c. 1900

Warwickshire Education Committee.

Balsall Street Central School.

Nr Coventry. ~~Department.~~

10 · ix · 1926

Chas George Viner has attended this School since 18. ii. 1924. He has been regular & punctual in attendance, well-behaved and attentive to his work; he has made steady progress.

His brother, Raymond Viner has been in regular attendance since 9. xi. 1925.

W F E Seeley.

Headmaster.

Chas Viner just promoted to Std IV

Raymond .. .. .. Senr Infants

Miss Steane's School, Moor Street, Earlsdon, 1931

Barker Butts School, 1931

Stoke Park Secondary School, May, 1936

COVENTRY EDUCATION COMMITTEE

COVENTRY TECHNICAL COLLEGE

Junior Technical School

FORM REPORT

Name *Jenks* Form *4A* Position *10* No. in Form *18*

Times present *136* Times absent *0* Next term commences *April 17th 1941*

Subjects	PERCENTAGES Term	Exam.	Position	Remarks	Master's Initials
English	69		5	Good.	D.M.B.H.
History & Geography	63		8	F. good. a quiet worker.	C.L.
Mathematics	74+		11	F.G.	H.J.Y.
Metalwork	56		13	Good. a little more speed.	J.B.
Woodwork	61		15=	Good.	W.S.G.
Engineering Drawing	56		10	Good	L.H.
Mechanics	60		15=		R.M.H.
Physics	80		4	Working very well	S.H.
Chemistry	66		11	Quite good.	K.H.D.
German	88		2	V. Good	F.B.

PHYSICAL EDUCATION	
Posture	*Shows improvement.*
Swimming	*He is now trying*
Gymnastics	*much harder & is far keener*
Games	*than before* J.H.D.

SCHOOL ACTIVITIES

CONDUCT	
Detentions	1
Report Cards	0
Corporal Punishment	0

Remarks *A good term's work.*

F. West *Headmaster.*

J. Wilson *Principal.*

Signature of Parent *D. Jenks.*

S3841/1000/2/40 (9)

Radford (temporary) Branch Library, October, 1931

Story hour at Stoke Branch Junior Library, 1948

Priory High School receiving instruction at Stoke, 1948

This library & its books are under the protection of the Boys & Girls of Coventry

King Henry VIII School Sports Day, 1954

Stoke Secondary Modern Boys' School Choir, 1955

Manor Park School, Cheylesmore, 1958

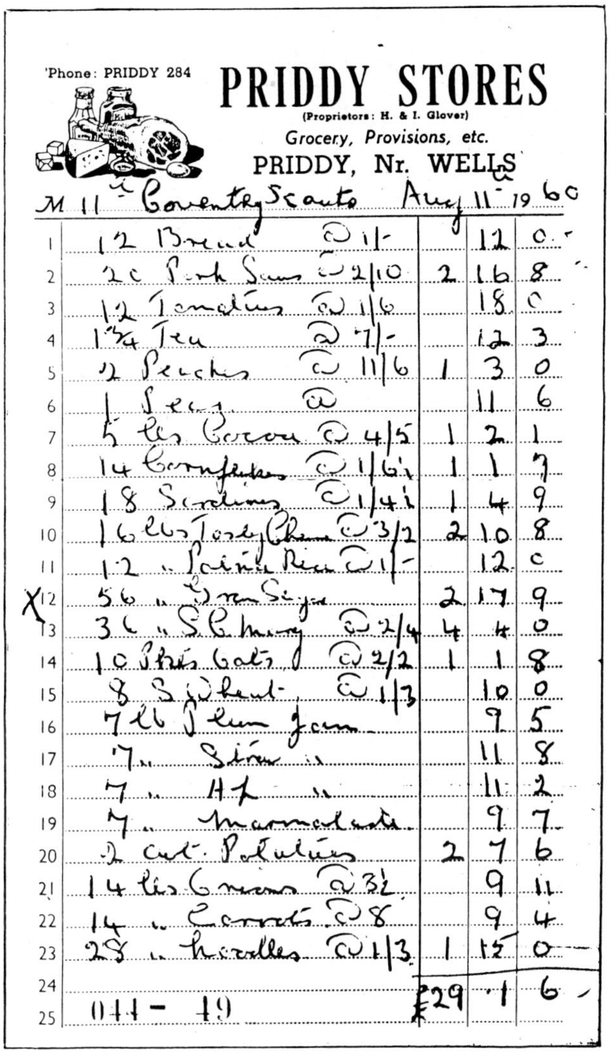

'Phone: PRIDDY 284

PRIDDY STORES

(Proprietors: H. & I. Glover)

Grocery, Provisions, etc.

PRIDDY, Nr. WELLS

M 11 – Coventry Scouts Aug 11 – 1960

1	12 Bread @ 1/-		12	0
2	20 Pork Saus @ 2/10	2	16	8
3	12 Tomatoes @ 1/6		18	0
4	1¾ Tea @ 7/-		12	3
5	2 Peaches @ 11/6	1	3	0
6	1 Veg. @		11	6
7	5 lbs Cocoa @ 4/5	1	2	1
8	14 Cornflakes @ 1/6½	1	1	7
9	18 Sardines @ 1/4½	1	4	9
10	16 lbs Tasty Cheese @ 3/2	2	10	8
11	12 " Patna Rice @ 1/-		12	0
X 12	56 " Gran Sugar	2	17	9
13	36 " S.C. Marg @ 2/4	4	4	0
14	10 Pkts Oats @ 2/2	1	1	8
15	8 S. Wheat @ 1/3		10	0
16	7 lb Plum Jam		9	5
17	7 " Straw "		11	8
18	7 " A.P. "		11	2
19	7 " Marmalade		9	7
20	2 cwt Potatoes	2	7	6
21	14 lbs Greens @ 3½		9	11
22	14 " Carrots @ 8		9	4
23	28 " Noodles @ 1/3	1	15	0
24		£29	1	6
25	011 – 49			

9th N. Coventry (Keresley) Company of Girl Guides' 21st celebrations, 1955

The Coventry Battalion of the Boys' Brigade, 1964

Alderman Harry Weston says "Au Revoir" to a group of Cheylesmore Scouts as they leave for camp in France in 1953

The staff of Wheatley Street Infants' School, 1895

THEY ALSO SERVE

COVENTRY never lagged behind other cities and towns in social work and it was in 1878, for example, that the founder of the Salvation Army, General William Booth, sent from London two women to begin the Army's work in the city.

The Marchioness of Reading formed in 1937 the WVS (later the WRVS) to perform a number of welfare duties that might arise from any national emergency. This service, in company with organisations such as the St John Ambulance and British Red Cross Society, to name just a couple, continue their excellent work.

The Coventry & Warwickshire Hospital came into existence in 1837, but it is surprising, considering the amount of infectious desease at that time, that the city's first isolation hospital was not opened until 1871.

A new library building was mooted in 1868 but this met with some resistance — "the money could be much better spent on a good soup kitchen." Only through the benefaction of Andrew Carnegie, the Scottish-American steel magnate, were the branch libraries at Earlsdon, Foleshill and Stoke built in 1913. Mr Carnegie was granted the honorary freedom of the city in 1914 for his generosity.

Meeting of Public Assistance Committee, c. 1930

City Council, 1928

City of Coventry Fire Brigade, 1911

The Standard Fire Brigade, c. 1910

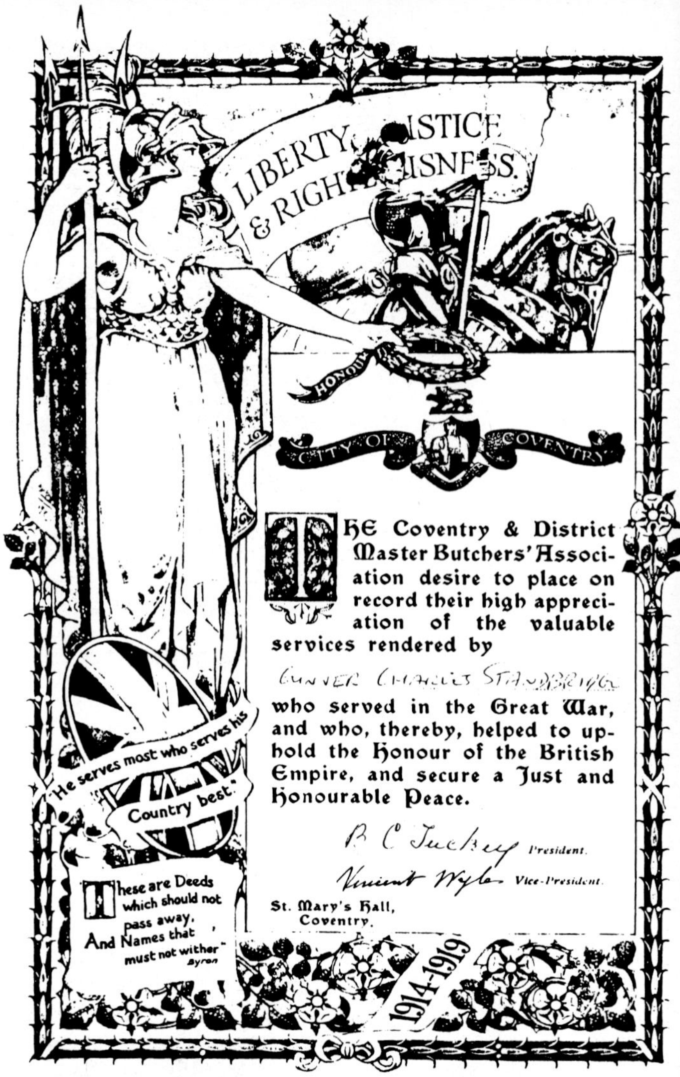

South Lancashire Regimental Band play outside Coventry Station, April 23, 1915

Coventry City Salvation Army Band, May 8, 1920

Barrack Square Police inspection, September 21, 1915

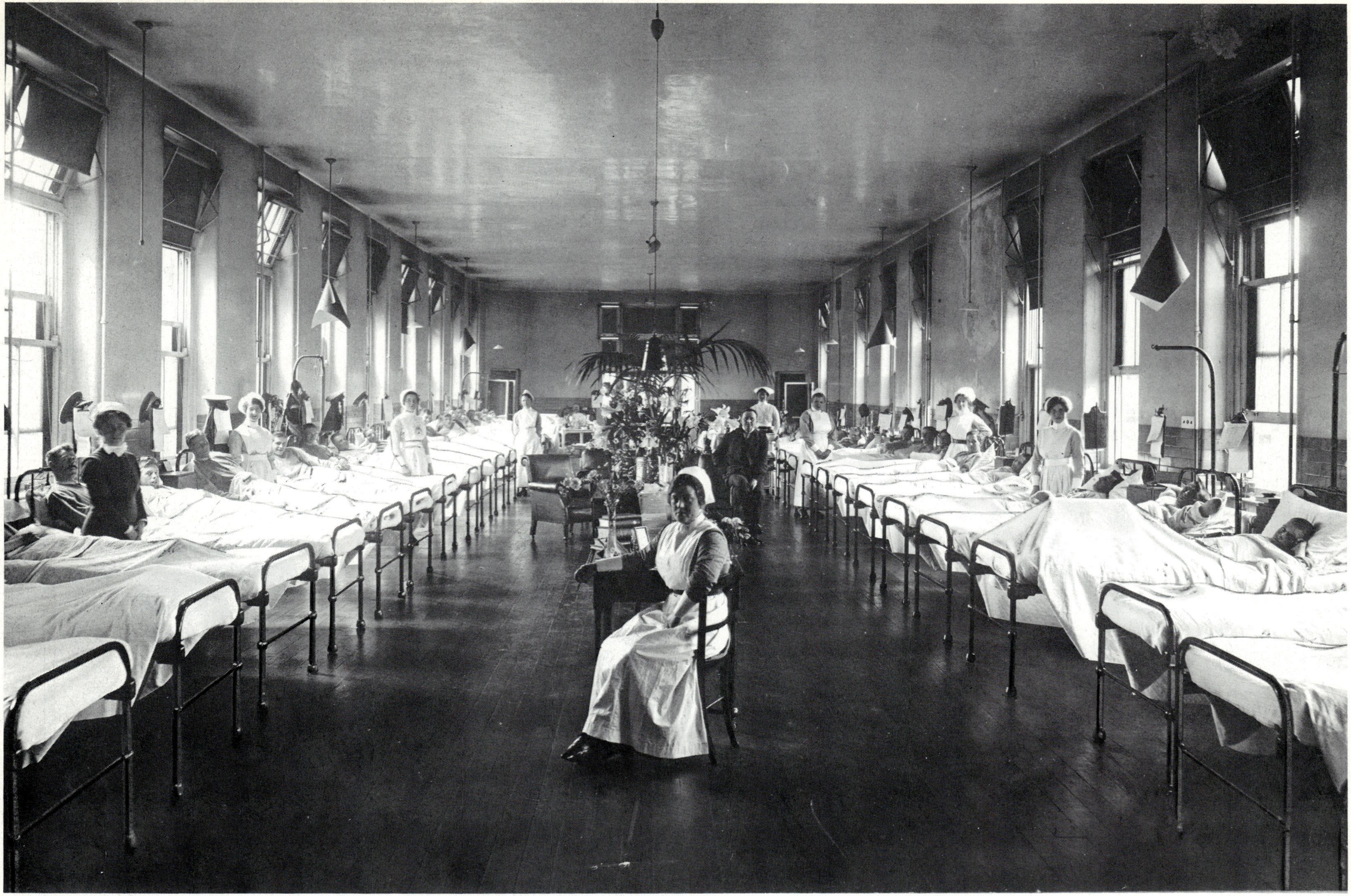

Wounded soldiers in Coventry and Warwickshire Hospital, 1916

Student nurses at Coventry and Warwickshire Hospital, Christmas, 1939

British Red Cross A team, c. 1960

t John Ambulance preparing for possibility of war, lexandra Theatre, Lower Ford Street, January, 1939

St John Ambulance Gaumont Cadets' 1st anniversary of Division, 1953

MEDICAL & SURGICAL

BIRTH CONTROL.—Absolutely Free: Five Books given away, post free, explains and solves our problems; containing information of vital importance to all married people, with Illustrated Catalogue of Surgical and Medical Goods.—Call or write: Le Brasseur Surgical Co., Ltd., Dept. W.T., 112, Little Park Street, Coventry. Head Office: 90, Worcester Street, Birmingham.

BIRTH CONTROL.—Books of advice by Dr. Marie Stopes. etc. Pamphlets free to adult callers.—Arkells, 24, Hales Street, and 47, Sandy Lane.

NO CURE—NO PAY!—Varicose Veins, Ulcers, Eczema Cured. End that agony and torment. Proof: "My ulcer is Completely Cured by the use of your treatment."—Mrs. Guest, 141, Tiverton Rd., Bournbrook, Birmingham. "It is over 5 years since you Cured My Ulcers, and as there has been no recurrence thought a second letter proving the permanence of your cure would be of interest to other sufferers."—Mrs. Huggett, 49, Melville Road, Maidstone. "Your treatment has Cured my ulcer and all pain has gone."—Mrs. Stanton, 65, Walsall Rd., Willenhall. Start your Cure To-day and call or write for Free Sample or 1/3 Trial Size and get Immediate Relief. Advice and Consultations Free. Open daily until 8 p.m., Saturdays 9 p.m. Official Contractors to the Birmingham Hospital Saturday Fund.—Le Brasseur Surgical Co., Ltd. (Dept. S.T.), 112, Little Park Street, Coventry.

RUPTURE. WHY SUFFER? Let us end your rupture worries for good and all. British doctors recommend our Super Light Appliance, and thousands of sufferers have found new hope through it. Why not you? To prove our words we send it Free on Trial. Safe, swift, and sure. Call or write to-day for Free Catalogue. You may be entitled to an Appliance Free if you are an Approved Society Member. Rupture Appliances from 4s. Advice and Consultations Free. Open daily until 8 p.m., Saturdays 9 p.m. Official Contractors to Birmingham Hospital Saturday Fund.—Le Brasseur Surgical Co., Ltd. (Dept. M.B.), 112, Little Park Street, Coventry.

WEAK MEN, GET VIGOUR! — Sample of Vi-Vims Free. Quick, speedy, and reliable remedy for lost vitality, and puts life instantly in weak glands and organs; age no barrier. Prices, 1/3, 3/-; assorted bottle of all strengths, 5/-; extra strong, 12/-; immediate results. "Rejuvenation" and Illustrated Catalogue Post Free, or call Le Brasseur Surgical Co., Ltd. Dept. C.B., 112, Little Park Street. Coventry.

St John Ambulance, Alfred Herbert Division, c. 195

Tea party for WVS members with the much-loved Pearl Hyde third from right, c. 1942

. . . and they also serve! Coventry & District Licensed Victuallers' Association visit Arthur Guinness Son & Co (Park Royal) Ltd, London, November 24, 1959

IN TOWN

DURING the Middle Ages, those ten or eleven centuries intervening between ancient and modern times, Coventry had dwelling-houses varying according to the social status of their inhabitants. The lord of the manor occupied his manor house just within the city walls at Cheylesmore; the rich merchants dwelt in their stone houses; timber buildings, well constructed, housed the middle-class craftsmen and shopkeepers; very basic, slumlike houses were the lot of the labourers.

Through good and bad times, neglect has taken its toll of the smaller dwellings. When aerial bombardment added destruction to decay it was inevitable that controlled demolition would also become necessary to accommodate the urgent need for re-planning.

Larger buildings, such as churches, have survived the bombs and the planners' designs. Ford's Hospital and Bond's Hospital, both with 16th century origins, are protected, being graded I and II respectively, and every effort will continue to be made to preserve them. A number of buildings in Spon Street are, in their turn, considered to be of special architectural or historic interest and are therefore protected.

Hearsall Lane/Broomfield Place, 1935

Barracks Square, January 26, 1950

Chapel of St James and St Christopher, Spon Street, 1898

Court 38 (North Side) Spon Street, c. 1957

A court in Bond Street due for demolition, October 26, 1956

Fleet Street, c. 1905

Fleet Street, 1952

Burges, 1930

Nos. 1-3 Burges, 1921

oss Cheaping, looking towards Bishop Street, 1892

onmonger Row, looking west from Bull Ring towards Cross Cheaping, 1935

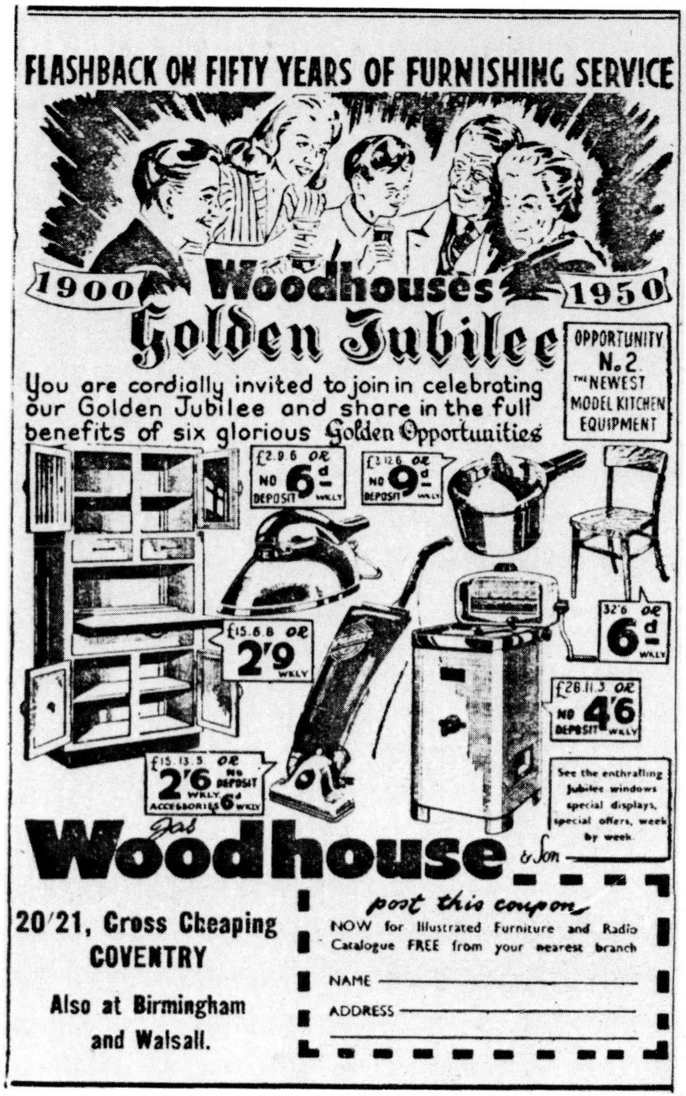

Cross Cheaping, looking towards Burges, c. 1936

Hales Street, 1935

Hales Street, 1952

Weston Street/Swanswell Street, c. 1966

Co-op Building, Smithford Street, 1933

Smithford Street, c. 1905

The Brightest and most Interesting Local Paper is

THE COVENTRY TIMES

And Warwickshire Journal,

PUBLISHED WEDNESDAY! 56 COLUMNS! ONE PENNY!

As an ADVERTISING MEDIUM The Coventry Times is unsurpassed. 1892

"WANTED" Class of Advertisements, ½d. per word, are inserted also in The Warwick and Leamington Times and The Nuneaton And Atherstone Times, without additional charge.

The Midland Daily Telegraph. Coventry Times and Warwickshire Journal. Warwick and Leamington Times. North Warwickshire Times.

No of Words.	*Midland Daily Telegraph.*	*Coventry Times W. & L. T. and N. W. T.*	Total No. of Insertions.	Price.
16	3 insertions	and Once in each of above.	six	1/3
16	6 ditto	ditto	nine	2/-
24	3 ditto	ditto	six	1/9
24	6 ditto	ditto	nine	2/6
30	3 ditto	ditto	six	2/3
30	6 ditto	ditto	nine	3/-

Chief Office:

18, HERTFORD STREET,

Warwick: 8, High St. Leamington: 20, High St.
Nuneaton: 124, Abbey St.

LONDON: 3, St. Bride Street, E.C.

Telephone No. 4 Coventry District.

WRIGHT'S DINING ROOMS,

68, Smithford St., Coventry.

ALSO

Park St., Walsall, and Dudley St., Wolverhampton.

GOOD DINNER 6D.

HOT · JOINTS · DAILY

From 12 a.m. to 10 p.m.

OUTDOOR ORDERS SUPPLIED.

A LA MODE BEEF,

OX TONGUE.

INVALIDS' BEEF TEA,

LADIES' DINING ROOMS.

TEAS! TEAS!! TEAS!!!

FROM 3D.

HOT SUPPERS.

Parties Catered for in large Room on Premises.
Separate Rooms for small Parties.

ESTIMATES GIVEN. 1892

Temporary shops, Smithford Street, c. 1946

A FOUR-FOLD INVITATION

From

THOMPSON-HUGHES CO.,

The City Stationers,

30 High Street & 23 White Street,

— COVENTRY. —

YOU CAN ADD TO YOUR PERSONAL STANDING

by always using high-grade Note paper when writing to your friends. How often one hears the phrase "I don't think much of her note-paper." Such a remark certainly lowers the writer in her friends' estimation. As surely as a shoddy or ill-fitting garment detracts from your personal appearance—so does cheap stationery detract from your personal standing. Think it over—is not this a matter worth your consideration? We believe we have just the papers to appeal to your taste, and shall be pleased to send or give you a Wallet of samples. Would you not like one of these?

LET US RELIEVE YOU OF THE WORRY

that is usually occassioned when Present-giving time comes round. As the day approaches you find yourself thinking "What shall I give So-and-so?" That will be your constant train of thought for day after day until you are perfectly sick of present giving. It is possible for you to avoid this worry by looking at our windows, or, better still, by coming inside and examining the charming selection at your disposal, at wonderfully cheap prices. It will give us pleasure to show you our stock, and remember, you are not under the least obligation to buy. Let us help you.

GIVE YOUR CHILDREN THE TIME OF THEIR LIVES

Toyland is the land of life for children! See how their eyes open with wonder and delight as they wander around some room crowded with toys! Here—at our White Street Branch—we have a splendid selection of Mechanical Toys, Engines, Trains, Motor Cars, Cinemas, Dolls, Bricks, Pets Stores, Soldiers, and a host of popular Table games. Everything that the bairns rejoice in will be found here galore, at prices just to suit your pocket. Watch the kiddies' faces as they gaze at our windows, and then—don't disappoint them—bring them in and give them their heart's delight.

WILL YOU WALK AROUND OUR ... IDEAL PICTURE PALACE

True, 'tis not as you might think—a palace of moving pictures—but for beauty and selection this wonderful show of PICTURE POSTCARDS is positively unequalled. There are pretty designs in hand-coloured Bromide Studies, Birthdays, Sentimental, Local Views, and the most screaming Comics you ever saw. A delightful variety always at your disposal. Will you come in and look around? See on your left and right the charming selection—the wonderful value!

1912

BROOKES's

118 Gosford Street, Coventry

CHEAPEST HOUSE IN MIDLANDS

FOR	FOR	FOR
Bags and Trunks	Ladies' Outfitting	Clothiers (contract)
Boots (Ladies')	Hosiery	Boot Factors
Boots (Children's)	Jewellery	Boxing Gloves
Boys' Clothing	Silverware, Plate, etc.	Sewing Machines
Gent.'s ditto	Baby Cars	Wringing Machines
Cutlery & E.-Plate	Drapers	Sheets, Blankets
Gent.'s Outfitting	Furnishers	Quilts, Bedsteads
Rain Coats	Bedding Manufacturers	Children's Outfitting

GENTLEMEN'S "READY-FOR-SERVICE" CLOTHING

Specialised

EVERYTHING IN GENTLEMEN'S OUTFITTING

Guaranteed

1913

A Blaze of Bargains always	*A Wave of Inciting Values*	*Values that always appeal*
Sole Proprietors of the Reg. "Phoebus" Silver & Gold Wristlets, Coventry made. Acknowledged by experts to be *the best*. Write for lists and particulars to Mail Order Department.	**Weighs 5 lbs.** Special Agent Coventry & District for the celebrated "Kozilyte" Fleece Overcoats. Warmth without weight. Write for lists. :: from **2 guineas.** ::	Sole agent for the "Britreyn" Rubberless Raincoats; embraces all the qualities of other celebrated makes. Write for speciallists. **35/- only.**

YOUR ORDERS will be esteemed; Prompt Attention and Despatch always. Before going elsewhere try us and send along.

118 GOSFORD ST. and 19 JORDAN WELL 118 GOSFORD ST.

Tel. 843. **COVENTRY.** Wire—BROOKES's OUTFITTERS

Broadgate, 1935

Broadgate, c. 1898

The new Cathedral under construction, March 6, 1961

High Street, 1910

Your Philco Radio Dealers

EVERY MODEL IN STOCK

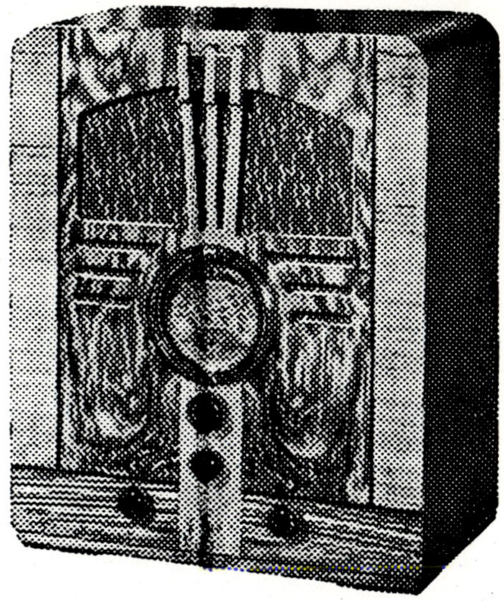

PAYNE'S

JESSON STREET, Coventry

(NOTE OUR ONLY ADDRESS)

Phone **2956**

1937

The oldest Newspaper in the County.

THE

COVENTRY STANDARD

Established July 20th, 1741,

Is the oldest, largest, and most widely circulated Journal in the neighbourhood. For more than a CENTURY AND A HALF it has been pre-eminently the leading Local and District Paper, and is the acknowledged Advertising medium in Coventry and throughout the numerous villages of North and Central Warwickshire, and the adjoining Counties of Leicester, Derby, and Stafford, where it circulates extensively.

FULL AND RELIABLE REPORTS!
MOST ADVERTISEMENTS!
LARGEST CIRCULATION!

Three Facts of the utmost importance to judicious Advertisers.

Published on Friday *(Market Day)* **& Saturday mornings.**
56 long columns. PRICE ONE PENNY.

THE COVENTRY MERCURY,

One Halfpenny. Published every Tuesday Evening. Four pages.
The mid-weekly Journal for Coventry and the District.

SPORT! FICTION! NEWS!

Terms for Trade Advertisements and all information may be had on application at the Office:

20, BROADGATE, COVENTRY.

Yorkist Meeting House, Little Park Street, 1920

Cow Lane/Little Park Street prior to demolition in 1937

Bull Ring and Butcher Row, seen from Ironmonger Row, 1935

Butcher Row, c. 1912

Butcher Row, 1935, prior to demolition to provide for a new Trinity Street

Butcher Row, 1934

Little Butcher Row, 1935

Hertford Street, 1929

Hertford Street, 1910

Hertford Street, c. 1910

West Orchard, 1912

Sanitary Pipes and Fittings. Blue Bricks and Staffordshire goods of all kinds. Floor Quarries, Roofing Tiles, Ridges, Chimney Pots, Cement, Lime. Gravel, Sand, Fire Bricks, Fire Lamps, etc.

WRITE OR 'PHONE FOR PRICES

G. W. JACQUES LTD.
BUILDERS' MERCHANTS
LYTHALLS LANE
COVENTRY
Telephone: COVENTRY 88045-6

Longford & Midland Concrete Co., Ltd.

(T. F. Bolton, A. G. Johnson and D. Pearson, Directors).

Specialists in Artificial and Reconstructed Stone Work of all kinds; also Hydraulic Pressure Flags and Kerbs, Rock Face Blocks, Breeze Blocks and Breeze Slabs.

WORKS:
BEDWORTH ROAD & GRINDLE ROAD WEST,
COVENTRY
Tel. 8236. SEND FOR QUOTATIONS

WARD BROS. & CO. (Coventry) Ltd.
COVENTRY'S LEADING BUILDERS' MERCHANTS
Tel.: 88065-6. Grams: 88065-6
Navigation Bridge, Stoney Stanton Road, Coventry.

GODIVA FIREPLACES grace countless homes in Coventry and district to-day. The installation of one of the many attractive designs is a sound investment yielding large dividends of pleasure and comfort.

Godiva Fireplaces Ltd.
32, EARL STREET
Nearly opposite Council House.
Telephone

Temporary shops, Earl Street, 1955

Coliseum Buildings, Jordan Well, c. 1928

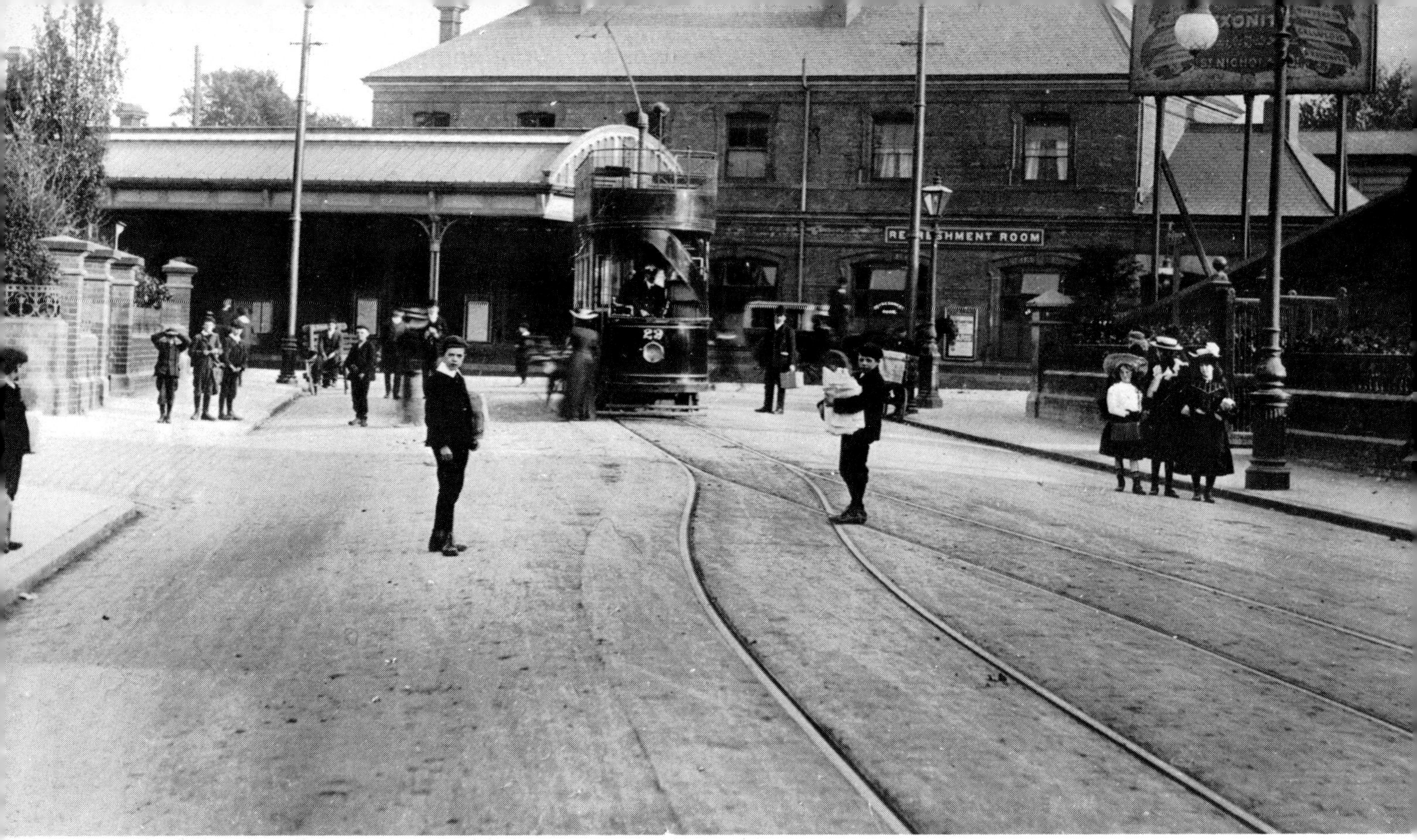

Coventry Station from Eaton Road, 1902

Gosford Street, 1916

Ansty Road, c. 1932

Binley Road, looking towards Far Gosford Street, c. 1910

Far Gosford Street, from Paynes Lane, January 4, 1960

ON THE MOVE

JAMES STARLEY (born in 1830) came to Coventry in 1861 and began to manufacture sewing-machines, but seven years later he was persuaded to make French bicycles with wooden wheels and iron tyres that soon earned the tag "bone-shaker." He improved these with steel wheels and solid rubber tyres, a large front wheel and a small rear one. So was born the "penny-farthing." Only the fittest of men could ride these, so Starley invented his tricycle. The "safety bicycle" soon followed for use by females as well as males and Coventry's flourishing cycle trade grew. The motor cycle and motor car industry in Coventry inherited a skilled workforce from the bicycle factories and further fame followed.

Not everyone could afford his own machine so the Coventry Tramways Co began in 1882 a steam tramway from the centre to Bedworth. Hills proved a problem until 1895 when steam was superseded by electricity. Later, Bell Green, Stoke, Chapelfields and Earlsdon were given routes. Motor buses started in 1912 and worked with trams until war damage to tracks in 1940 saw the tram system being abandoned.

Dual carriageways, flyovers, bypasses and motorways assured the motor car speedy journeys and Coventry a thriving trade.

The railway came to Coventry in 1838, connecting with London and Birmingham and later, in 1850, the line to Nuneaton was completed.

In July, 1935, when flying was attracting much interest, the city established an aerodrome at Baginton, on land that had been municipally owned since 1897. This wisdom and foresight is evident today in a fine, well-run airport.

James Starley, c. 1875, founder of the cycle trade in Coventry

"SWIFT" CYCLES

MAY BE PURCHASED UPON OUR

GRADUAL PAYMENT SYSTEM.

This System is instituted to enable anyone to become possessed of a High-class Machine by payment at fixed dates, of such small sums as may be convenient.

THE FOLLOWING ARE SOME OF THE MOST IMPORTANT FEATURES:

The Perfect Privacy of the System.

Every order is taken in strict rotation, no preference given. Only ONE quality of each class of Machine. No distinctive marks.

No difference whatever (except the usual Cash Discount) between the Cash Buyer and the adopter of the GRADUAL PAYMENT SYSTEM.

NO INTEREST! NO FINES! NO PUBLICITY! NO TROUBLE!

THE COVENTRY MACHINISTS' COMPANY, LIMITED.

ORDER FORM ATTACHED.

1893

Coventry-made Starley bicycles on show at Crystal Palace, 1900

Early examples of the motor-makers' art, The Motor Manufacturing Co Ltd, c. 1898

THE NEW PENNINGTON AUTOCAR.

I am now prepared to accept orders in large quantities for my New Patent Autocar,
AS ILLUSTRATED ABOVE.

THIS IS THE ONLY MACHINE:

Made to carry four people, fitted with a seven horse-power motor.
That will *not* blow up, or where passengers do not run risk of being set on fire.
(All machines using a carburetter, or lamp, are liable to blow up, or be set on fire, at any moment, sacrificing life and property.)
That can carry its full load up a steep hill at a high speed.
That can be stopped on a steep hill, and start again uphill with a full load.
That can run up a long hill without emitting forth smoke or steam.
That can run for several hours without using lubricating oil on running parts.
That can run over tram lines at any angle with perfect safety.
That is fitted with unpuncturable tyres.

Is the lightest machine built to carry four people.
Is the strongest machine built to carry four people.
Is the best running machine for all-round work.
Is ready to start at a moment's notice.
Has less loss of power between motor and driving wheel than any other machine built.
Has less odour than any other machine built.
Has less vibration than any other machine built.
Has less noise than any other machine built.
Why buy an Autocar that you may have to set aside in a few days, owing to the contravention of the new Board of Trade Regulations.
Orders also accepted for three-wheeled machines to seat two people.
And for four-wheeled Victorias, to seat either two or four people, with overhead hood.

For Prices and Full Particulars regarding their sale in Great Britain, address—

E. J. PENNINGTON, Motor Mills, COVENTRY.

Coventry Motor Club, Charterhouse, c. 1902

A Riley Fore-car of 1903, inspected by the Library Committee, 1955

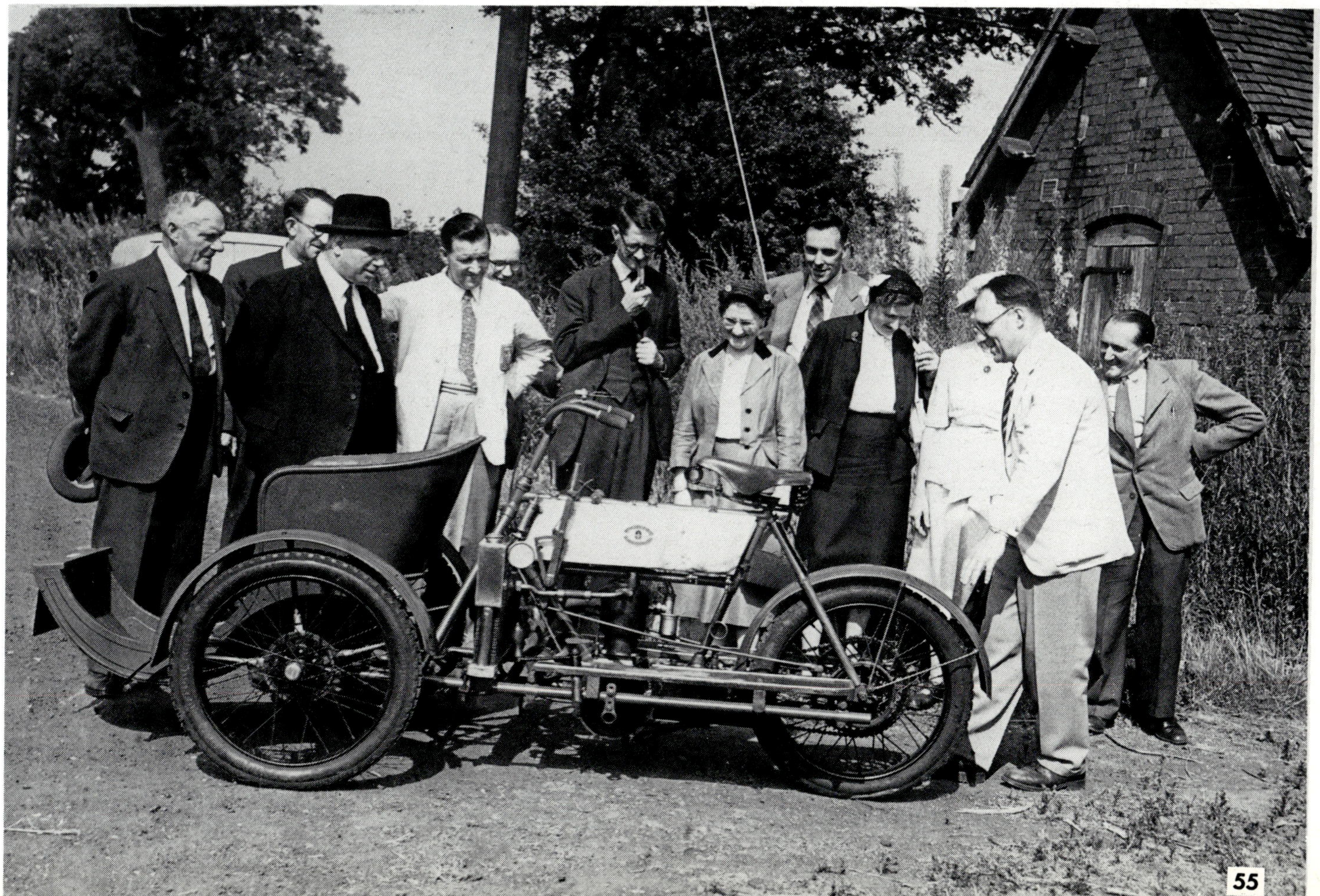

Coventry Station yard, showing Daimler cars and a Daimler bus, 1921

Calcott Bros Ltd, 1921

Horse bus, c. 1900

Maudslay bus in Walsgrave Road, 1914

Humber Hotel, c. 1914

Open-top motor bus in use on Stoke Heath/Hearsall Common route, c. 1919

Corporation Transport, c. 1927

Dennis bus, used for country services, Pool Meadow, 1936

Coventry Transport

Serving a population of 215,000, operate

TRAMCAR SERVICES:

No. 1	Bedworth	Cov. Station	every 10 minutes
„ 2	Longford	Broadgate	„ 5 „
„ 5	Bell Green	Cov. Station	„ 10 „
„ 6	Broad Street	Broadgate	„ 5 „
„ 8	Uxbridge Avenue	Broadgate	„ 8 „

BUS SERVICES:

No. 1	Stoke Heath	Maudslay Road	every 10 min.
„ 2	Green Lane	Radford	„ 10 „
„ 3	Stoke Aldermoor	Hen Lane	„ 6 „
„ 4	Stoke Heath	Coundon	„ 10 „
„ 5	Binley	Coundon	„ 10 „
„ 6	Lenton's Lane or Alderman's Green	Earlsdon	Hourly
„ 6	Walsgrave	Earlsdon	every 10 min.
„ 7	Allesley	Pool Meadow	„ 12 „
„ 8	Tile Hill	Pool Meadow	„ 15 „
„ 9	Broad Lane	Broadgate	„ 20 „
„ 10	Brownshill Green	Pool Meadow	„ 30 „
„ 11	Glendower Avenue	Pool Meadow	„ 10 „
„ 13	Willenhall	Pool Meadow	„ 20 „
„ 14	Inner Circle		„ 30 „
„ 16	Keresley	Pool Meadow	„ 40 „
„ 17	Baginton	Pool Meadow	„ 40 „
„ 18	Burton Green	Pool Meadow	Approx. hourly
„ 19	Berkswell	Pool Meadow	Approx. every 2 hours

Subject to adjustment in accordance with traffic requirements.

CITY OF COVENTRY TRANSPORT

AT YOUR SERVICE

CAMERA PRINCIPIS

1937

Vernon Street/Paynes Lane, c. 1935

Broadgate, c. 1938

Tram conductresses, Broadgate, 1915

Coventry Station, c. 1879

Coventry Station, October 23, 1959

October, 1945

AT WORK

THE author of "Robinson Crusoe," Daniel Defoe, visited Coventry in the early part of the 18th century and he was most complimentary about the diligence and expertise of local craftsmen. "The city is large and populous, having a great trade consisting chiefly of the weaving of tammy (worsted cloth) and ribbons. It is the very image of the City of London," and he went on to describe the beauty of the timber buildings and quaint streets.

The making of cloth was foremost in trade, employing weavers, drapers, tailors, dyers, fullers and shearmen. Until modern industry brought fame and fortune to the city with the manufacture of cycles, motor cycles, cars, aeroplanes and electrical equipment, early metal trades provided an admirable training ground for future artisans. Among these older trades were needle-making, brass, pewter and gold fashioning, watches and clocks. Millers, brewers and victuallers were always in demand as were the products of the glass and tile makers, the hatters and the glovers.

Telephone 766. THE 1912

Northampton Brewery Co. Ltd.,

ARE NOTED FOR THEIR

SPECIAL BRIGHT ALES

IN CASK AND BOTTLE.

Caterers especially are requested to try these Beers.

Wines and Spirits of the finest quality.

Offices and Stores for Coventry and Leamington Districts:

5 St. Nicholas Street, Coventry.

E. C. GOULSTON, Local Manager.

Great Horseless Carriage Company works, c. 1897

Swallow workers, 1930

Swallow factory, 1930

Armstrong Siddeley demonstration car (for self-change gearbox), Holyhead Road, c. 1932

Maudslay Motor Co Ltd, Park Side, c. 1910

Testing re-conditioned engines at Triumph, July 3, 1959

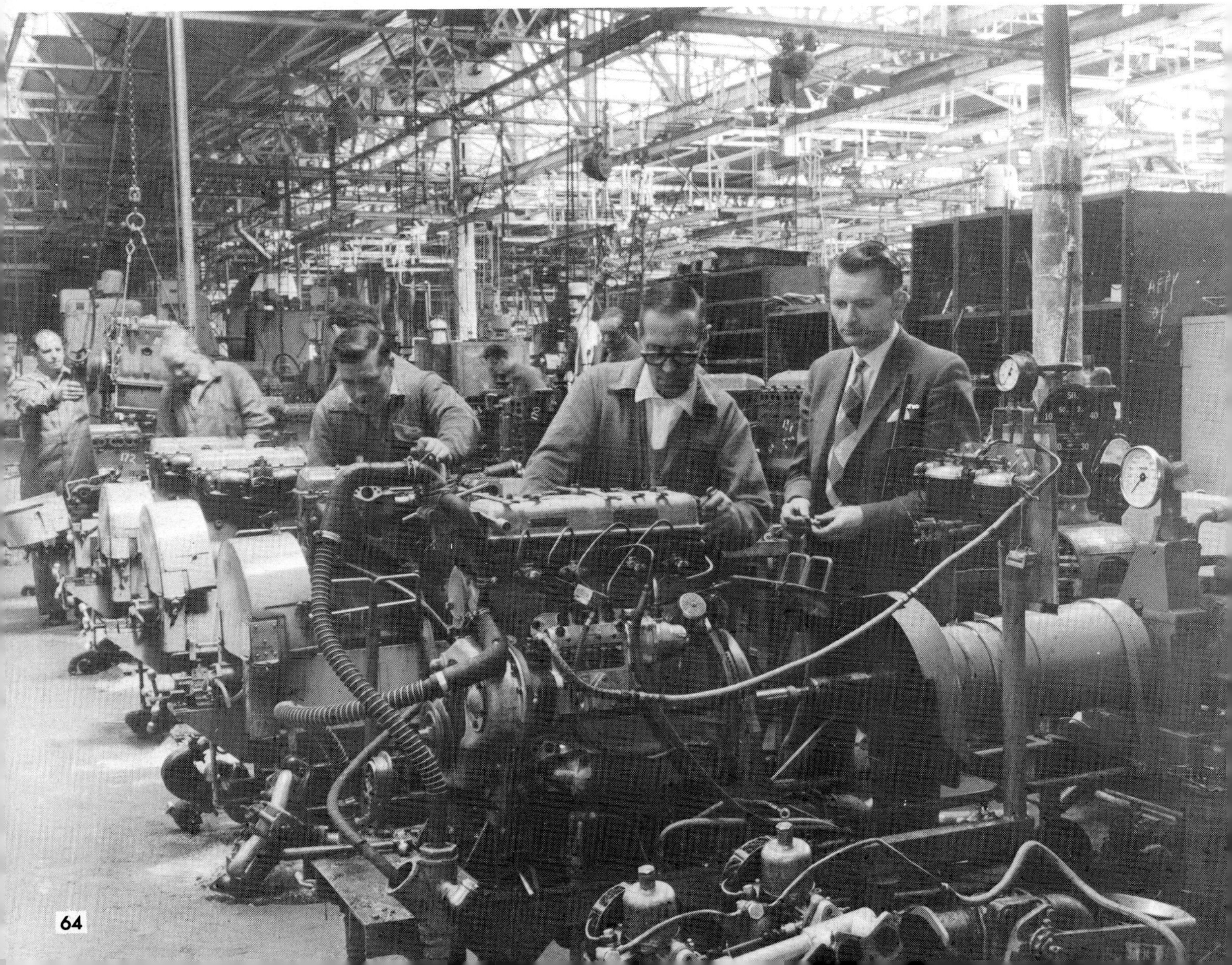

Massey-Ferguson, c. 1956

Daimler, c. 1914

Alvis, 1930

Alvis, 1920

Calcott Bros Ltd, April, 1921

The Foundry, Coventry Evening Telegraph, 1959

Coventry Evening Telegraph, 1960

White & Poppe Ltd, c. 1908

GEC 1908

MAGNETO CALL TABLE TELEPHONE.

K **8085**

Comprising a Hand Microtelephone, with "Hunningscone-Deckert" Transmitter and Double-pole "Ring" Receiver, Nickel-plated Ornamental Cradle Switch, Induction Coil, Generator with two extra large Permanent Magnets, Polarized Call Bell, Four-conductor Flexible Connecting Cord, and Wall Rosette with Terminals and plate-type Lightning Arrester with perforated Mica Insulation. All external metal parts Nickel-plated and Lacquered. The Magnets are provided with four Rubber Feet, to prevent damage to desk or table.

Price £5 0 0

Peel-Conner Telephone Works (later GEC), c. 1922

Workers leaving GEC Telephone Works, 1939

Errington Watch Works, Holyhead Road, c. 1920

"Brink," the last horse of the Coventry Co-operative Society, with head stableman and driver, April 23, 1956

Market Square, c. 1910

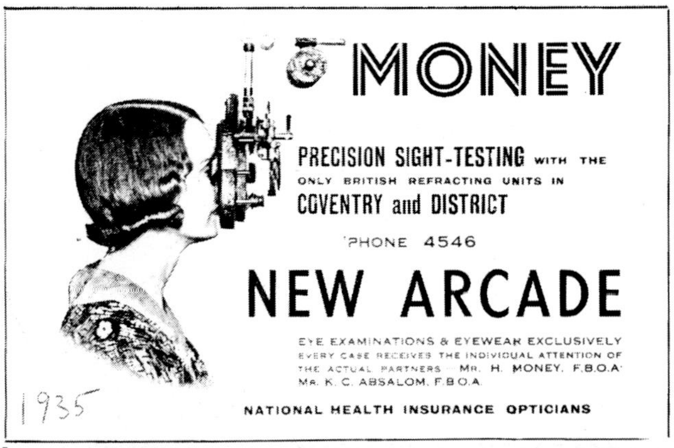

C. Standbridge, 19 Victoria Street, c. 1913

Turrall's, Leicester Causeway, 1907

54 Spon Street, 1941

AT PLAY

FOR centuries poaching for salmon or game was rife though forbidden by national and local laws, yet in Coventry bull-baiting and bear-baiting were openly encouraged by the city authorities. Cock-fighting was not favoured by them yet it survived even into living memory. Archery was not allowed in the streets towards the end of the 15th century, so special mounds or butts were constructed for safe practice. Barkers' Butts Lane and The Butts mark the sites of two of these. By the early 16th century mere craftsmen were forbidden to play bowls, quoits or football because they would then tend to neglect their work upon which their livelihood depended. Horse-racing became popular in the 18th century, meetings being held in the park adjoining the city. Coventry Football Club (Rugby Union) was founded in 1873 and did not lose a game until the last match in the 1876/77 season. Early games were played at the Old Bull Fields until the move to The Butts in 1880. After World War I came the move to Coundon Road. The Golf Club came into being in 1887, with courses at Pinley Fields and Whitley Common. The move to Finham Park took place in 1908.

Coventry & North Warwickshire Cricket Club was set up in 1851. Prominent past members included Lord Kenilworth and R. E. S. (Bob) Wyatt, the former Warwickshire and England cricket captain.

Coventry City Football Club Ltd (the Sky Blues) was formed by employees of Singer and played under that Company's name until 1898. Coventry City had slipped to the newly-created Fourth Division by 1952, yet, under Mr Derrick Robins (chairman) and Mr Jimmy Hill (manager), the team eventually swept thrillingly into the First Division. The Club's record attendance of 51,455 was achieved at the home game against Wolves on Saturday, April 29, 1967. In 1987 the Sky Blues won both the FA Youth Cup and the FA Cup.

Cinemas in Coventry, as elsewhere, were most popular and the super-cinemas, for example The Gaumont Palace (opened in October, 1931) and The Rex (opened in 1937), were greatly patronised. Prior to the Second World War local firms who had flourishing social clubs for their young, skilled workers provided value-for-money entertainment. The less fortunate paid 1/6d or half-a-crown (7½p or 12½p) for a dance at the Rialto or attended a 2d (1p) open-air dance, known as a "hop," at the Red House in Red Lane.

Coventry City FC, Division III Champions, 1963/64

Cheering crowds acclaim Coventry City FC, Division II Champions, 1966/67

Coventry Football Club (Rugby Union), 1945/46

Iliffe Athletic Club Rugby XV, 1904/5

Courtaulds Hockey Team, c. 1920

Warwick Road Cricket Club, champions of the Coventry & District Free Church Cricket League, 1904/5

Godiva Harriers, 1913

Coventry cyclists, 1892

Alfred Herbert Cycling Club, 1932

The Bees, 1966

Members of the Coventry Motor Club at Kenilworth, 1925

Opening of Priory Street Baths, 1894

Gosford Swimming Pool, August 8, 1955

HIPPODROME *Theatre* **COVENTRY**

Direction .. .. S. H. Newsome
General Manager and Licensee .. .. .. Harry Bannerman
Acting Manager .. .. R. Neal
Public Relations .. .. Guy David
Director of Music .. .. .. W. E. Pethers
Box Office (Mrs. I. O'Neill) open 10 a.m. to 8 p.m. ('Phone 3141)

COMMENCING AUG. 25th, 1947
FOR TWO WEEKS
6-15 **TWICE NIGHTLY** 8-30

BERNARD DELFONT presents—

Laurel & Hardy in Variety

1. OVERTURE
   W. E. Pethers, and the Coventry Hippodrome Orchestra. MARCH " All Set " (*Belton*)
2. THREE REDHEADS
   Moments of Dance
3. BOB LLOYD & BETTY
   Popular Comedy Team
4. OLGA VARONA
   Australia's Queen of the Air
5. CARL & ROGER YALE
   The Song Writing Comedians
6. SLIM RHYDER
   Komedy Kapers
7. INTERMISSION
   W. E. Pethers and the Coventry Hippodrome Orchestra. SOUVENIRS de FRANCE (*Hanmer*)
8. THREE REDHEADS
   More Steps in Rhythm
9. JACK and MARY KINSON
   " You'll Be Surprised ! "
10. MACKENZIE REID & DOROTHY
11. STAN LAUREL & OLIVER HARDY
    Hollywood's Greatest Comedy Couple
    Assisted by Harry Moreny
12. CYNTHIA & GLADYS
    Beauty and Balance

Forthcoming Attractions

September 8th **Twice Nightly 6-15 & 8-30**
Langham Productions & Hyman Zahl present—
ISSY BONN
in his New Road Show
" BIG BROADCAST OF 1947 "
with
BILLY RHODES & CHIKA LANE :: SIKI & SON
THE TWO MOVERS :: VIVIAN
RAY BURNS :: JACK MARKHAM :: BERI SHAW
LES JOHNSON :: GORDON ROLFE :: FLORENCE WHITELEY'S ZIO ANGELS

September 15th **Nightly 6-45** **Mats. Thurs. & Sat. 2-30**
PRIOR TO LONDON PRODUCTION !
A New Musical with two of America's foremost Singing Stars
LYN CEELEY and **LORRAINE BRIDGES**
in
" GARDENIA LADY "
ANTONY HOLLES :: BERNARD HUNTER
ANNE DOONAN :: IAN COLIN
JACK MAY :: IVAN BEROLD :: WINEFRIDE INGHAM
And Full Supporting Company

SUNDAY, SEPTEMBER 7th at 7-0 p.m.
CAMPOLI
with the
CITY OF BIRMINGHAM ORCHESTRA
Conductor : GEORGE WELDON
Prices 2/6d to 8/3d. :: Box Office Now Open

COMING SHORTLY :—
The 'OLD VIC' Theatre Company
HARRY GREEN in **" FIFTY-FIFTY "**
INTERNATIONAL BALLET
THE DANCING YEARS etc.

EMPIRE THEATRE

MONDAY, NOVEMBER 11th, 1918, FOR SIX DAYS.
T 3 and 6.30—EXCEPTING THURSDAY, 3, 6.30 and 8.30.
THE FILM BOOKING OFFICES, LTD., PRESENT

"RAFFLES"

THE AMATEUR CRACKSMAN.
A SEVEN-PART PRODUCTION OF THE FAMOUS NOVEL AND PLAY BY E. W. HORNUNG, Starring

JOHN BARRYMORE

Supported by The Latest Comedy & Topical Programme.
EVERY EVENING AT 8.30 (THURSDAY EXCEPTED),

WAR SERVICE LECTURES

By NAVAL and MILITARY OFFICERS. See Special Bills.

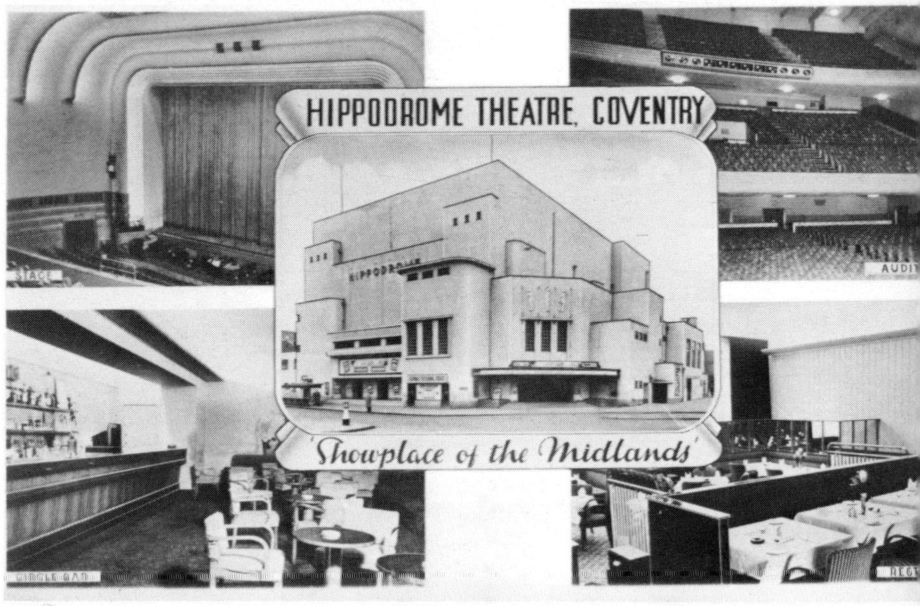

NEW HIPPODROME

Phone 3141-2-3 COVENTRY BOX OFFICE OPEN 10 to 10
CAR PARK OPPOSITE
MONDAY, APRIL 3rd. 6.30 Twice Nightly 9.0

UNIT PRODUCTIONS LTD. present
THE GREAT ANGLO-AMERICAN SHOW

HAWAIIAN PARADISE

INCLUDING

THREE PETERS SISTERS

65 STONE of HARMONY and SONG

SENSATIONAL SINGING STARS OF EDDIE CANTOR'S "ALI BABA GOES TO TOWN"

MAURICE COLLEANO

THE WORLD'S GREATEST ACROBATIC COMEDIAN
WITH
BONAR, TORIO, GEORGE & RUBYE

THE 4 JACKS

SENSATIONAL SINGING SAILORS

MARQUEEZ

EXOTIC EASTERN DANCER

8 VALDETTES

GLAMOROUS DANCING GIRLS

GEORGE BOLTON

THE NEW GAGSTER

OLSEN & JOY

ROMANCE IN DANCE

SMEDDLE BROS.

WHO MAKE IT TAKE IT AND SHAKE IT

The Ludo Press, 373, Earlsfield Road, London, S.W.18.

The Coventry Repertory audience on the hottest night of the year, Hales Street, July 12, 1934. The play was "Ten Minute Alibi"

he Barron Knights at the Locarno, 1965

HIPPODROME *Theatre* **COVENTRY**

Mon., Tues., Wed., Fri., 7.30 Thurs. and Sat., 5.0 & 8.0.

BETTY ANN DAVIES

in

A STREETCAR NAMED DESIRE

FRANCES HYLAND — THEODORE BIKEL
and WILLIAM SYLVESTER.

The Sensational Play Direct from the Aldwych Theatre, London.

OCTOBER 2nd. For Two Weeks. Nightly, 7.30. Mats. Thurs. & Sat., 2.30
Prince Littler presents the Famous Musical Play "WHITE HORSE INN."

Advance booking open now for "OKLAHOMA," commencing Tuesday October 24th, for Four Weeks (No telephone bookings accepted for this attraction.) Prices: 12/6 8/6, 7/6, 3/6. (Permanent Bookings kept for first week only unless we are otherwise notified.)

Advance Booking now open for Pantomime — "JACK AND JILL."

Box Office Open 10.0 a.m. to 8.0 p.m. —— 'Phone Coventry 3141.

FOLESHILL **ROXY** PHONE 2389

THURSDAY, SEPTEMBER 28. FOR THREE DAYS.

FRANCHOT TONE — ANNE BAXTER:

FIVE GRAVES TO CAIRO (A) At 6.25, 9.10.

Also: Eddie Dean .. .. .. HAWK OF POWDER RIVER (U). At 5.23, 8.5.

HOLBROOK LANE. 'Phone 88565. **LYRIC** FREE CAR PARK.

THURSDAY, FRIDAY, SATURDAY. Continuous from 2.30-10.30.

JACK WARNER — JIMMY HANLEY — PEGGY EVANS:

THE BLUE LAMP (A)

At 3.40, 6.15, 9.0. And FULL SUPPORTING PROGRAMME

STANDARD LUXURY CINEMA

THURS. FRI. SAT. Two Big Pictures. Chums Club Saturday at 10 a.m.

Abbott and Costello:
MEET THE KILLER (A)
Boris Karloff, At 2.15, 5.20, 9.0

Yvonne de Carlo, Scott Brady:
The Gal who took the West (U)
Technicolor, At 3.45, 7.20.

PLAZA SPON END · PHONE 4822

RIVOLI LONGFORD · PHONE 88325

THURSDAY, Sept. 28, for 3 Days. AT BOTH THEATRES.

JOEL McCREA — ALEXIS SMITH — ZACHARY SCOTT:

SOUTH OF ST. LOUIS (A) (Tech.) At 2.38, 5.50, 9.0. Rivoli 6.10, 9.15.

Also: David Niven, Jane Wyman: KISS IN THE DARK (A). At 4.24, 7.39. Rivoli 4.50, 7.55.

CHUMS' CLUB SATURDAY, 10 a.m.

ODEON TEL 3429

FAR GOSFORD STREET
THIS WEEK
Jean Simmons, Michael Rennie and an All-Star Cast in:
TRIO (A)
Showing at 2.30, 5.40, 8.56
FATHER MAKES GOOD (U). This Modern Age No 37 The True Face of Japan (U).

GLOBE TEL 3813

THIS WEEK.
Ricardo Montalban, Sally Forest:
MYSTERY STREET (A)
Times: 2.25 5.40 8.55.
Also: — Beg, Borrow or Steal (U).
Times: 4.16 and 7.30.

REGAL TEL 88312 · **ASTORIA** TEL 2056

Regal from 2.35. THURS. FRI. SAT. Astoria from 2.15. No Matinee Friday.

ROBERT YOUNG — BETSY DRAKE:

ELLEN (A)

Regal at 2.50, 5.55, 9.0. Astoria 2.40, 5.50, 8.50.

Also: Emlyn Williams and Eve Arden .. .. .. THREE HUSBANDS (A).

Last Complete Performance: Regal 7.25, Astoria 7.20.

Hippdrome Orchestra, 1945

GAUMONT THEATRE & CAFE RESTAURANT COVENTRY TEL 20421

TO-DAY. At 2.0, 5.20, 9.0.
ROBERT NEWTON — KATHLEEN HARRISON — SUSAN SHAW:
WATERFRONT (A)
James Mason and Margaret Lockwood . . . . . THE MAN IN GREY (A).

OPERA TO-DAY—Cont. 9.30 a.m.-10.45 p.m.
The thundering epic of grit and glory—the mighty drama of a handful of heroes and their date with destiny.
BACK TO BATAAN (A)
with JOHN WAYNE — ANTHONY QUINN — BEULAH BONDI
NEXT WEEK — NORTH-WEST MOUNTED POLICE.

ALEXANDRA TO-DAY— Cont. 1.0 - 10.45.
Adventure, thrills. Pulsating with stark terror in the dark interior of the jungle.
ALBERT DEKKER:
DR. CYCLOPS (A)
In Technicolor.
Drama and thrills galore in sensational drama of a girl bullfighter.
Ray Milland, Dorothy Lamour:
TROPIC HOLIDAY (U)
NEXT WEEK — Barton MacLane: UNKNOWN ISLAND.

EMPIRE COVENTRY Phone: 3600
TO-DAY FROM 12.45. Last Complete Programme 7.15.
CLARK GABLE — LORETTA YOUNG:
KEY TO THE CITY (A)
At 2.15, 5.30, 8.45.
Richard Arlen, Patricia Morison: THE BLACK STALLION (U). 1.0, 4.10, 7.30
HOLY YEAR (U). Commentary by Wilfred Pickles.

FORUM 'Phone 1583. Walsgrave Road. 'Bus Route No. 6. Large Car Park
THURSDAY, FRIDAY, SATURDAY. Continuous from 2.0 p.m.
BARBARA STANWYCK, JAMES MASON, VAN HEFLIN, AVA GARDNER:
EAST SIDE, WEST SIDE (A)
M.G.M.'s star-studded battle of the (un)fair sex. At 3.0, 5.50, 8.45.
With Full Supporting Programme.

SAVOY 'Phone 3374. Radford Road. 'Bus Routes 2, 14, 16. Large Car Park.
THURSDAY, FRIDAY, SATURDAY. Continuous from 2.0 p.m.
Shirley Temple, Barry Fitzgerald, Lon McCallister:
PRIDE OF KENTUCKY (U)
Technicolor. At 2.35, 5.40, 8.50.
Ronald Reagan, Virginia Mayo:
THE GIRL FROM JONES BEACH (A)
At 4.10, 7.20.

CROWN THEATRE
THURS. FRI. Cont. 2.0. SAT. 4.30.
James Mason, Margaret Lockwood:
THE WICKED LADY (A)
Also: John Blyth:
IT'S A WONDERFUL DAY (U)
Captain Marvel—Episode 11.

PRINCE OF WALES
THURSDAY, FRIDAY, SATURDAY.
LOUIS HAYWARD, JANET BLAIR, EDGAR BUCHANAN:
THE BLACK ARROW STRIKES (U)
Also: William Bishop:
ABOVE ALL LAWS (U).
Times: Thurs. Cont. 2.30. Friday 6.0. Saturday 5.0.

PALLADIUM
THURS. FRI. SAT. Mary Beth Hughes:
INNER SANCTUM (A)
Also: John Carradine: C MEN

IMPERIAL THEATRE
THURS. FRI 6 p.m. SAT. 5 p.m.
Douglas Fairbanks, Richard Greene:
THE FIGHTING O'FLYNN (U)
Also: INTO THE STRAIGHT (U)

The Rex - Coventry

CONTROLLED BY	THE PHILPOT CIRCUIT
MANAGING DIRECTOR	H. T. A. PHILPOT
DIRECTORS	H. T. A. PHILPOT & G. W. R. PHILPOT
GENERAL MANAGER	HARRY HEATH
RESIDENT MANAGER	RUPERT TODD
ARCHITECT	ROBERT CROMIE, F.R.I.B.A.

SOUVENIR PROGRAMME OF THE OFFICIAL OPENING
BY
THE RIGHT WORSHIPFUL THE MAYOR OF COVENTRY
(ALDERMAN A. H. BARNACLE, O.B.E., J.P.)

MONDAY, 8th FEBRUARY, 1937

SAVOY CINEMA & BALLROOM

RADFORD, COVENTRY
TEL. 3374

CONTROLLED BY	THE PHILPOT CIRCUIT
MANAGING DIRECTOR	H. T. A. PHILPOT
DIRECTORS	H. T. A. PHILPOT & G. W. R. PHILPOT
GENERAL MANAGER	HARRY HEATH
RESIDENT MANAGER	NORMAN R. BRUNT
ARCHITECT	T. D. GRIFFITHS

SOUVENIR PROGRAMME OF THE OFFICIAL OPENING
BY
CAPTAIN W. F. STRICKLAND, M.P.

SATURDAY, 2nd JULY, 1938

EVENTS

A CHARTER of incorporation was granted to Coventry by Edward III in 1345, being the first of its kind in the country, giving powers to the corporation to elect a mayor, bailiffs and other leading citizens to preside over the city. In 1451 Henry VI raised Coventry to a County of the City, this status being removed in 1842 whilst still retaining the title "City." It became a County Borough in 1888 and, in 1953, coronation year, Queen Elizabeth II conferred the dignity of a Lord Mayoralty on the city. She laid the foundation stone of the new cathedral on March 22, 1956. Earlier, on Christmas Day, 1946, a radio exchange programme was put out by the BBC linking Coventry with the continental cities of Arnhem, Caen, Stalingrad and Warsaw, which led to exchange visits between Coventry's Mayor and those of Arnhem and Caen. This friendly gesture prompted similar exchanges between other towns and cities in Western Europe.

Spon Street, New Year's Eve, 1900

Albany Road, Earlsdon, July 4, 1904

Coventry Station, November 21, 1959

Tenants ejected from condemned property in Well Street, 1912

Closure of Little Butcher Row by the Mayor, Alderman Payne, January 1, 1936

Visit of Queen Mary and Princess Royal to inspect the munition works. At Canon Baillie's home, Vicar's Croft, Davenport Road, September 18, 1917

The Duke of York (later King George VI) comes to open the new Council House in Earl Street, June 11, 1920

Princess Elizabeth (now the Queen) opens the rebuilt Broadgate, May 24, 1945

Part of the crowd awaiting the arrival of King George VI and Queen Elizabeth, Broadgate, April 5, 1951

CITY OF COVENTRY

CIVIC DINNER

Thursday, 29th August, 1946

AT

THE BRITISH RESTAURANT
ALBANY ROAD, COVENTRY

To mark the occasion of
the Visit of

The Commanding Officer, Officers & Men of

H.M.S. "Argonaut"

Coventry's Adopted Ship

7 p.m.

Counc. J. C. LEE-GORDON, J.P.
Mayor

SOUVENIR

OF THE

OPENING

OF THE NEW

HUMBER WORKS

AT

COVENTRY

March 12th, 1908.

The occasion is the laying of the foundation stone for the Empire Theatre, June 30, 1906. The famous actress Ellen Terry sits in the back of the car

Opening of the War Memorial Park, 1921

Installation of Mrs Pearl Hyde as the first lady Lord Mayor of Coventry. This was the first televised mayor-making ceremony anywhere, May 23, 1957

Lord Iliffe lays the foundation stone of the new Coventry Evening Telegraph building in Corporation Street, November 21, 1957

Opening of Corporation Street, June 13, 1931

Coach-and-four outside the Old Posting-House, High Street, c. 1900

Godiva procession in Broadgate, 1907

Outing of cycle and motor workers, 1900

Wayzgoose (an outing) for Coventry printers, c. 1910

Tank Bank Week, Broadgate, 1918

Coventry Carnival, 1928

Godiva Pageant and Carnival, 1929

White & Poppe outing to Holt Fleet, June 1909

Armstrong Siddeley Band and contingent near No. 2 Gate prior to the unveiling of the War Memorial in the Memorial Park, 8 October 1927

CITY OF COVENTRY
EDUCATION COMMITTEE

OPENING OF THE NEW
TECHNICAL COLLEGE BY
HIS ROYAL HIGHNESS
THE DUKE OF YORK, K.G.
DECEMBER 10th, 1935

Charter celebrations, 1945

Staff and guests at the prizegiving at The Birches (residence for nurses of the Keresley branch of Coventry & Warwickshire Hospital), 1952

British Thomson Houston workers visit Newdigate Colliery, 1960

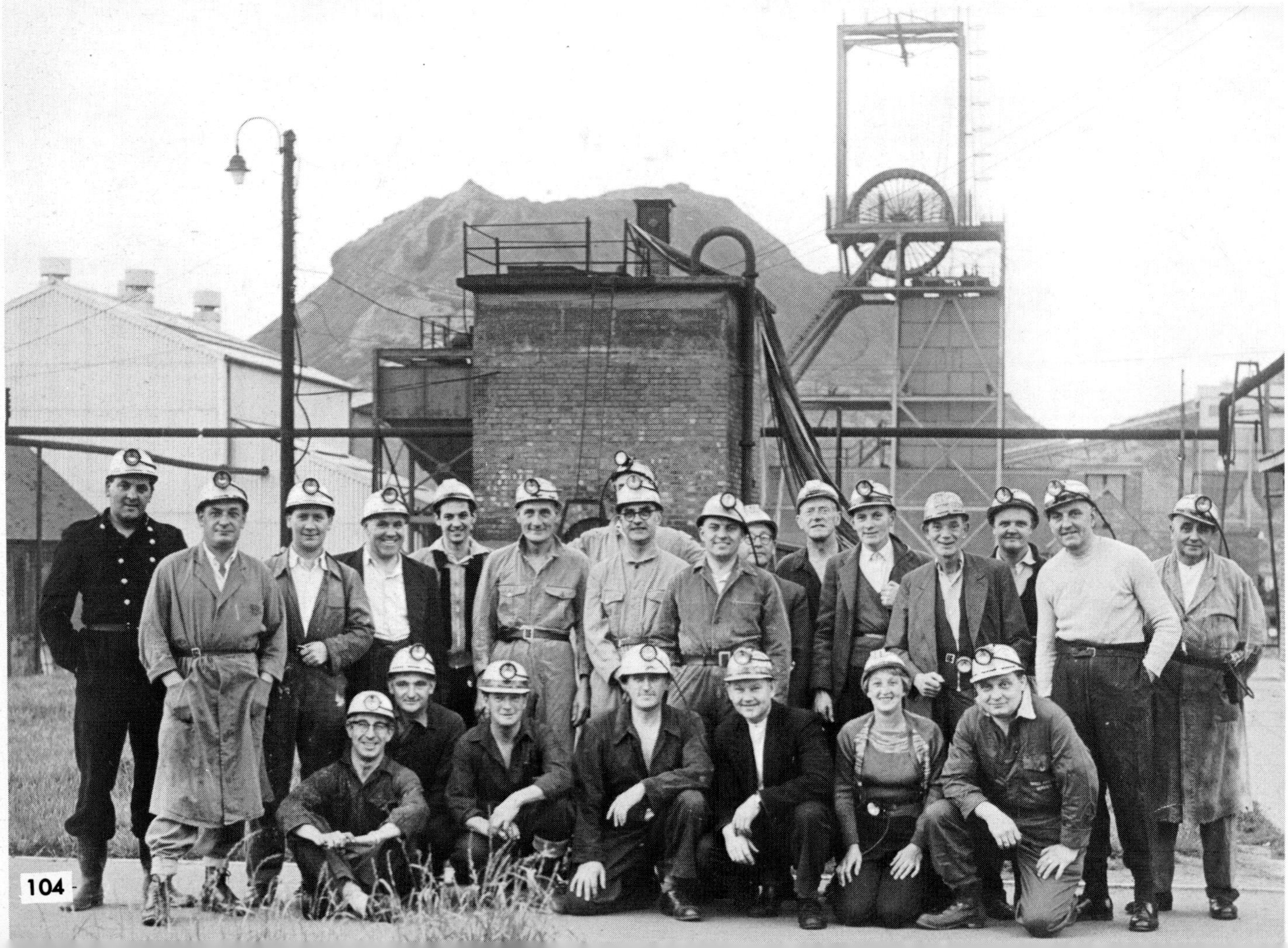

GREEN AND PLEASANT

THE fact that population numbers within the city appear to be falling slightly points to the availability, within quite short distances, of green fields, farmlands and rural villages which tempt city dwellers to set up home outside the tight inner-city boundaries. The hatred of ribbon development along roads going out from the cities in the 1930s caused Coventry and Birmingham to confer together with the county of Warwick with a view to preserving an undeveloped area, a green belt, around the two cities. Thankfully this policy is being maintained, for under the Town & Country Planning Act (1932) the city gained powers to this end.

Rear of Ford's Hospital, October 6 1931

The city seen from Greyfriars Green, c. 1885

The Fair on Pool Meadow, c. 1920

The Forge, Coat of Arms Bridge Road, Stivichall, c. 1860

Coat of Arms Bridge, Stivichall, 1943

The Grove, Kenilworth Road, c. 1910

Canley Milk Bar, August 12, 1969

Bedworth Road, Longford, c. 1935

FOR SALE & WANTED

ADANAC CO., Harefield Road, Coventry.—Garages, Greenhouses, or Bungalows. Property Repairs. Garages from £6; Sheds from £3 10s., erected free. Telephone 2526.

A BARGAIN in Portable Buildings is not necessarily the cheapest. Try the oldest firm in the district for quality.—Fellows and Son. Canley Gates. 'Phone 2774.

A BARGAIN in Garages and Garden Sheds; best and cheapest in city. Inspection invited. Cash or terms.—Pollard's Portables, Myrtle Grove, Moor Street, Earlsdon. 'Phone 60500.

A SELECTION of Sheds, Garages, and Green houses at the Sectional Shed Company, Brighton Street, Coventry. Open evenings 7 to 8 o'clock, and on Saturday afternoons.

A SHANKS' Built-to-Last Sectional Building—value for money; no regrets. Showgrounds: Durbar Avenue and Cheveral Avenue; open Saturday afternoons.—E. O. Shanks and Sons, Ltd., Lockhurst Lane, Coventry.

ALLEN'S CASH STORES is the Shop to Exchange. Your Lux Toilet Coupons and get their full value. Also finest Safety Matches, 7½d. per dozen. Finest Soap Flakes, 5½d. per lb.—17, City Arcade; and 6, Market Arcade

ALL types of Garages and Sheds; prices to suit all —42, Hall Green Road, Bell Green. Open Sunday.

A.R.P. FOOD STORAGE.—Biscuits in half tins from 2/8 each, including tin.—City Biscuit Co., 24, City Arcade.

BIRD CAGES.—Best value in the city.—Barford and Co., Ltd., Bishop Street, Coventry.

BEAMAN, Parkstone Road, Foleshill, near the Gasworks. Any class of Timber supplied; orders and inquiries, large or small, have personal attention. Prompt delivery anywhere. Tel 8102.

"Never for a moment, during the thirty-one years we have been working, have we devoted our attention to any form of localised machine. We took into consideration every world condition that exists."

—HARRY FERGUSON

To meet the needs of farmers everywhere

—under all conditions

The famous Ferguson Tractor—prime mover of the Ferguson System.

ONE TRACTOR, one system, one agricultural method for farmers everywhere, under all conditions. That is the contribution of the Ferguson System of *complete* farm mechanisation. It is a contribution that gives farmers their first real chance to farm as they have always wanted to farm.

What is the Ferguson System?

The Ferguson System consists of two parts: the Ferguson tractor and a Ferguson implement. Simple 3-point linkage and hydraulic control — both manual and automatic — co-ordinate the action of the tractor and implement. They work together as a single unit to provide these six advantages:

1. *Traction without excess built-in weight.*
2. *Penetration without weight.*
3. *Hydraulic depth control of the implement.*
4. *Automatic protection from hidden obstructions.*
5. *Easy attachment of implements in one minute.*
6. *Tractor front end stays down—even up-hill.*

The sum total of these advantages is easier farming, better farming, more profitable farming. Today, farmers in 56 countries are proving that the Ferguson System enables them to produce more food at less cost — regardless of the size of their holdings, the nature of the soil or the type of crops grown.

Ferguson tractors and implements for world-wide distribution are produced by the most modern methods and equipment. Tractors for the eastern hemisphere are produced in the 90-acre factory of The Standard Motor Co. Ltd., Coventry, England, and implements by foremost British manufacturers. Farmers in the western hemisphere are supplied from the great new 72-acre plant of Harry Ferguson, Inc., Detroit, Michigan, U.S.A.

FERGUSON SYSTEM

N.4

It will pay you, too – to FARM WITH FERGUSON

Swanswell, 1906

STERLING METALS LTD

Coventry

SPECIALISTS IN CAST IRON CYLINDER BLOCKS AND HEADS

TELEPHONE: COVENTRY 89031 (6 lines) TELEGRAMS: STERMET PHONE COVENTRY

THOMAS WILKINSON,

Loom Maker and Machinist,

PAYNE'S LANE,

COVENTRY.

LOOMS FOR WEAVING—

Plain and Fancy Ribbons. Bookmarks and Portraits. Gold and Silver Lace, Army & Navy Lace. Coach Lace and Furniture Trimmings. Elastic Webs, Girthing Webs, &c.

ALL KINDS OF ACCESSORIES. AGENT FOR JACQUARD MACHINES.

AWARDED 5 HIGHEST PRIZE MEDALS AND DIPLOMAS.

Peterboro' 1882. **London, 1884.** **Cork, 1883.**

Medal Ribbons, Monograms, Badges, &c.

W. H. GRANT,

FOLESHILL, NEAR COVENTRY.

Devices of every Description to Order.

MANUFACTURER OF FANCY SILK GOODS,

Silk Handkerchiefs, Silk Brace and Garter Webs,

LADIES' TIES, BOOK-MARKS, SILK PORTRAITS, EXHIBITION SOUVENIRS, FLOSS FRINGES, TASSELS, &c., &c.

ACKNOWLEDGEMENTS

(for providing photographs, for encouragement and numerous other favours)

Neil Allen; Alvis Ltd; Jo Ault; Austin Rover; Mary and Jim Boulton; Dave Carpenter; Coventry Division of the West Midlands Police; Coventry Evening Telegraph Staff; Coventry Fire Station; Coventry Local Studies Library; Beryl and Ted Cross; Jim Garside; GEC Telecommunications Ltd; Clive Hardy; John Harrison; Jaguar Cars Ltd; Pat and John Jenks; Anne Jennings; Margaret and Jack Lathbury; Massey-Ferguson; Philip Murphy; Museum of British Road Transport, Coventry; Ken Narborough; Ray Norton; Pat Pearson; Victor Price; Gil Robottom; Rolls-Royce Heritage Trust; the Salvation Army; John Spencer; Stoke Park School and Community College; Gordon Stretch; Edna and Raymond Viner; Ron Williams.

Please forgive any possible omissions. Every effort has been made to include all organisations and individuals involved in the book.